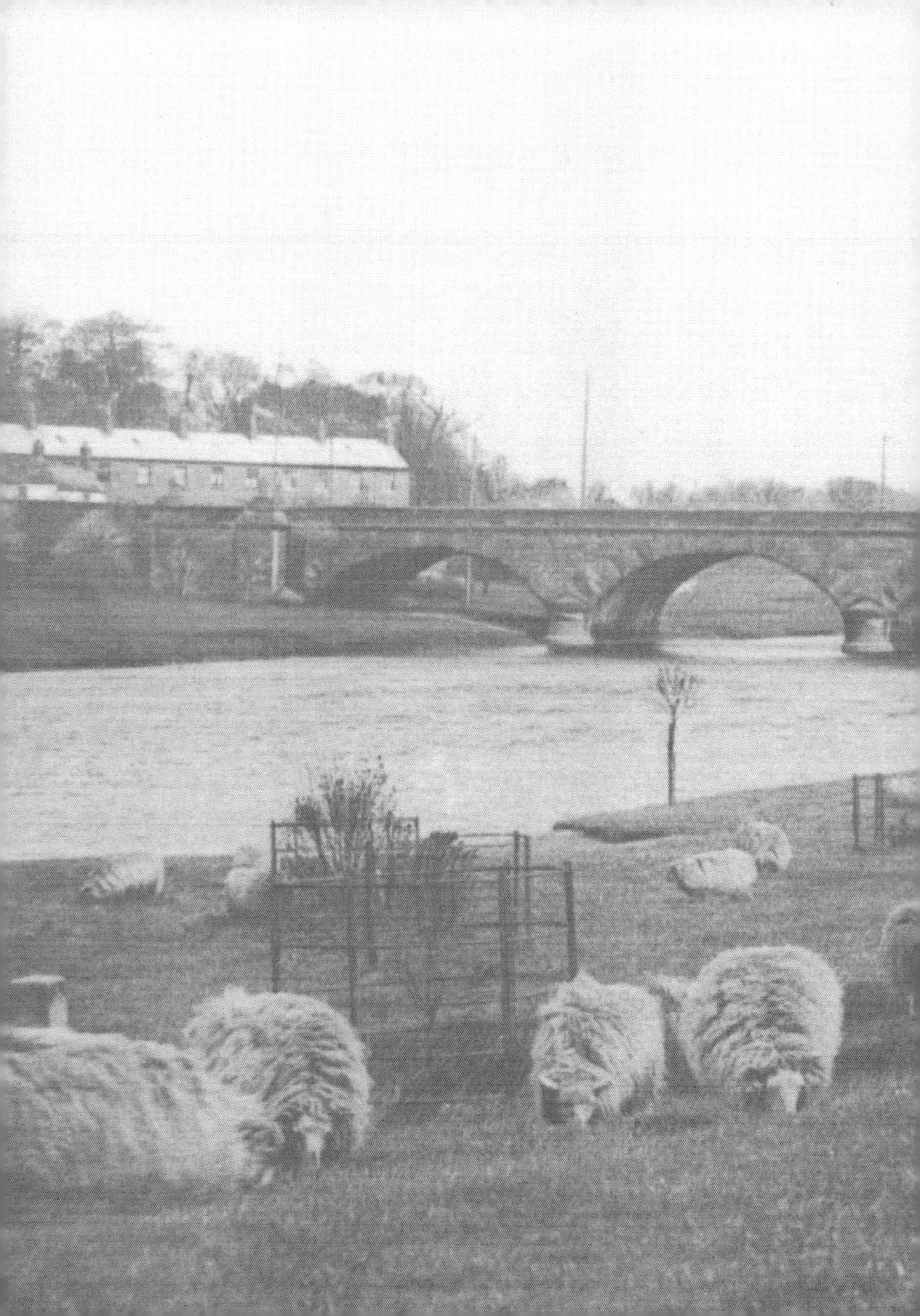

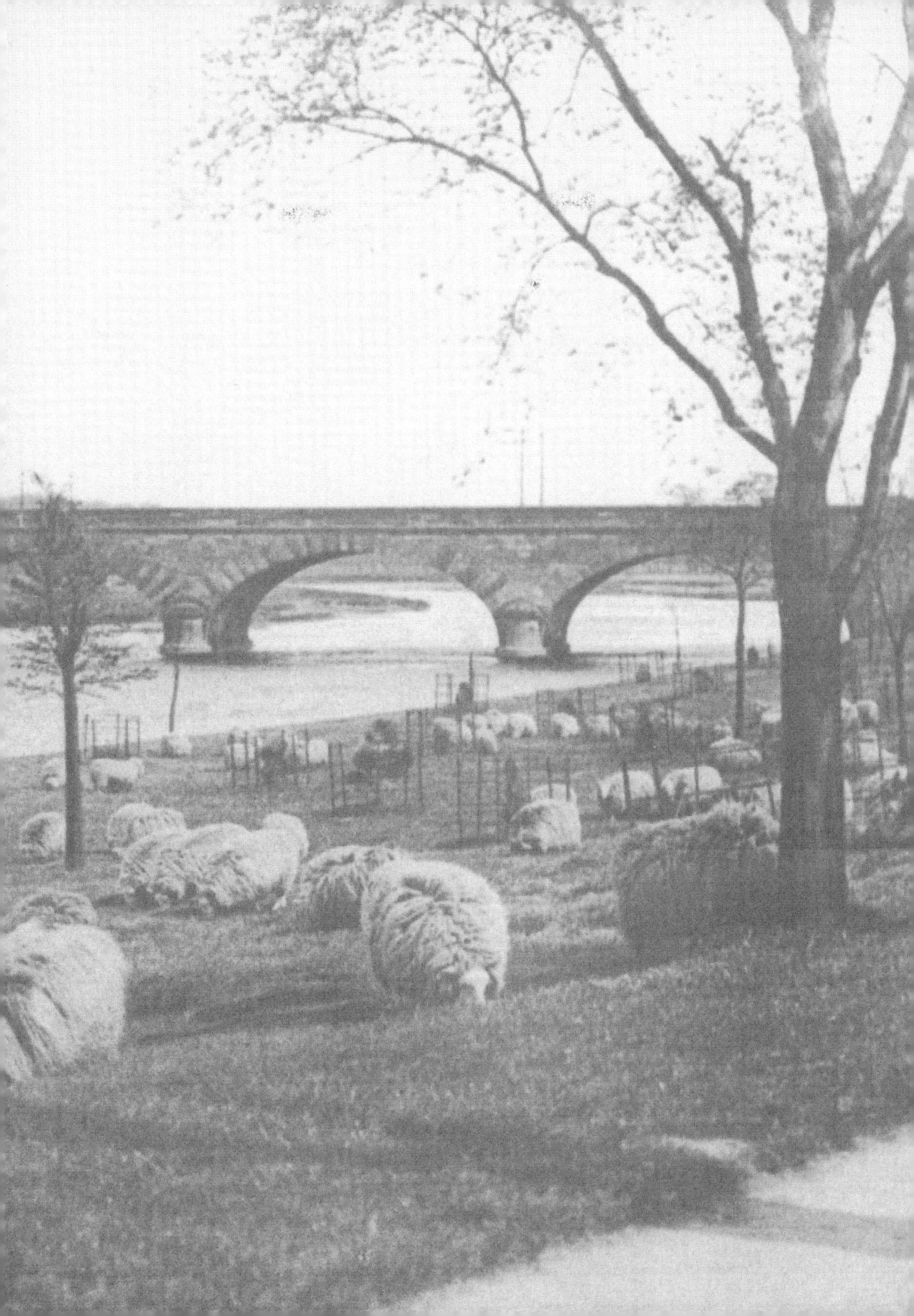

A CENTURY of
CARLISLE

Jimmy Dyer, Carlisle fiddler and character, pictured here in Old Grapes Lane in 1900. On Sundays Jimmy would sit beside the River Eden for most of the day, chatting to passers-by. He died at his father's pub in Stanwix in 1907.

A CENTURY of CARLISLE

CHARLIE EMETT AND
J.P. TEMPLETON

The History Press

First published in 2000 by Sutton Publishing Limited

This new paperback edition first published in 2007

Reprinted in 2013 by
The History Press
The Mill, Brimscombe Port,
Stroud, Gloucestershire, GL5 2QG
www.thehistorypress.co.uk

Copyright © Charlie Emett and J.P. Templeton, 2000, 2007, 2013
Copyright © 'Britain: A Century of Change', Roger Hudson, 2000, 2007, 2013

All rights reserved. No part of this publication may be reproduced, stored in a retrieval system, or transmitted, in any form or by any means, electronic, mechanical, photocopying, recording or otherwise, without the prior permission of the publisher and copyright holder.

The authors have asserted the moral right to be identified as the authors of this work.

British Library Cataloguing in Publication Data
A catalogue record for this book is available from the British Library.

ISBN 978-0-7509-4909-5

Front endpaper: Eden Bridge, Carlisle, 1909.
Back endpaper: Carlisle cross topped by its lion facing Scotland, English Street, *c.* 1987.
Half title page: Queen Victoria Statue in Victoria Park, Carlisle.
Title page: Carr's Works Brass Band, *c.* 1946.

Typeset in 11/14pt Photina.
Typesetting and origination by
Sutton Publishing.
Printed and bound in England.

Mayor Phillips at a Carlisle school on Empire Day 1923.

Contents

FOREWORD BY THE MAYOR OF CARLISLE, COUNCILLOR RAY KNAPTON	7
BRITAIN: A CENTURY OF CHANGE *Roger Hudson*	9
CARLISLE: AN INTRODUCTION	15
THE DECADE OF PRIVILEGE	19
THE DECADE OF PATRIOTIC FERVOUR	31
THE BITTER-SWEET '20S	41
THE NECESSITOUS '30S	49
THE VIOLENT '40S	61
THE TEENAGE '50S	71
THE SPACE AGE '60S	81
THE DEPRESSIVE '70S	91
THE PROUD '80S	101
FIN DE SIÈCLE	111
ACKNOWLEDGEMENTS	121

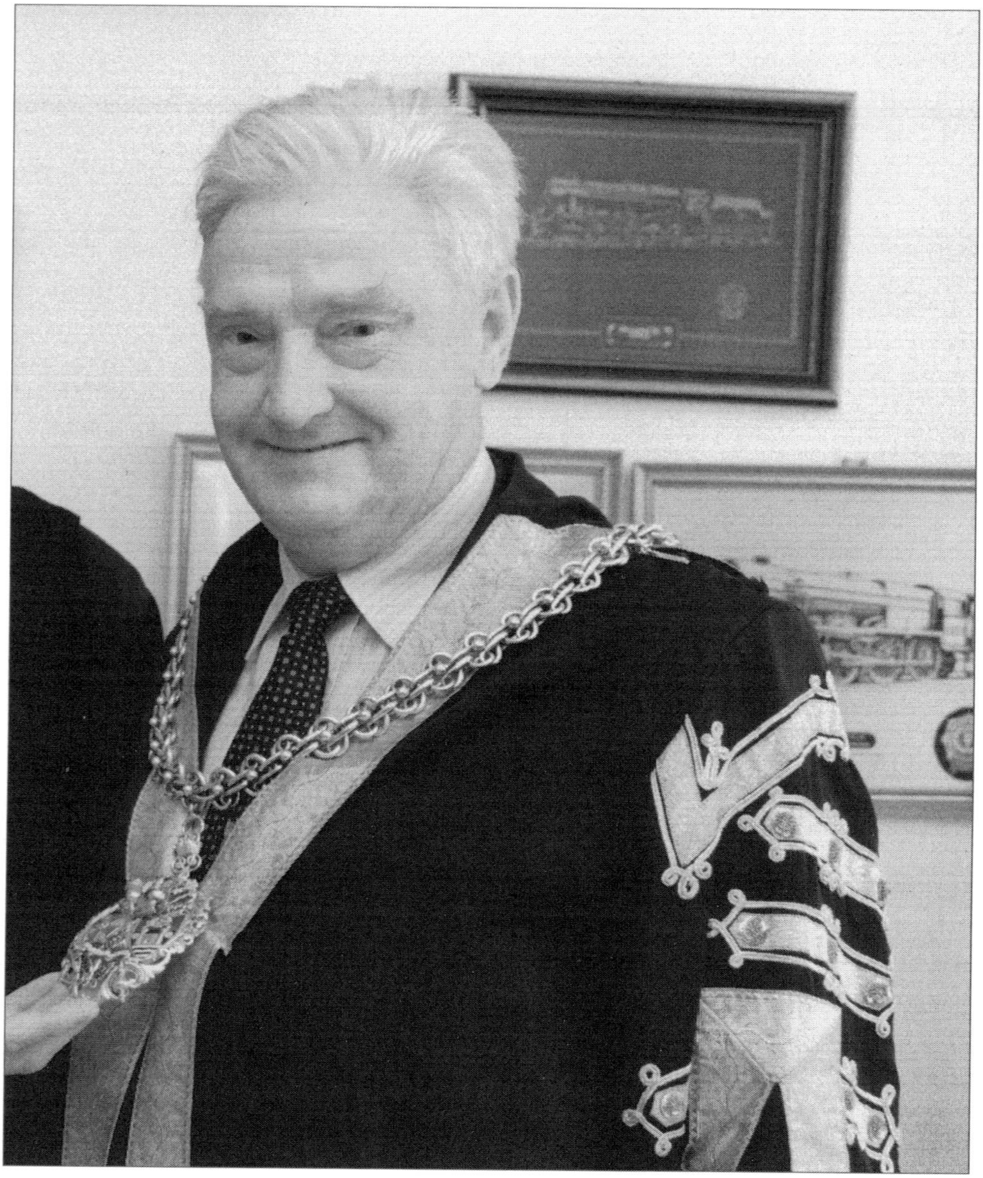

Foreword

COUNCILLOR RAY KNAPTON

The situation of Carlisle is extremely fine: it stands on gentle rising ground, in the midst of extensive fertile meadows, terminated by the distant mountains, and watered by the Rivers Eden, the Caldew, and the Petteril.

The former two of these rivers flow on different sides of the City and form the ground plot on which the city stands.

Along the banks of these three rivers, their slopes and contiguous meadows afford a number of pleasant walks to the inhabitants of our city.

This is a small attempt on my part as Mayor of this city to put into words what I think of Carlisle.

Mayor of Carlisle

A CENTURY *of* CARLISLE

Autumn, Keats' season of mists and mellow fruitfulness, in Bitts Park. The lady pushing the pram is Mrs Anne Templeton and her elder daughter, Frances, is at her side. Her younger daughter, Elizabeth, is out of sight, in the pram.

Britain: A Century of Change

Two women encumbered with gas masks go about their daily tasks during the early days of the war. (*Hulton Getty Picture Collection*)

A CENTURY of CARLISLE

The sixty years ending in 1900 were a period of huge transformation for Britain. Railway stations, post-and-telegraph offices, police and fire stations, gasworks and gasometers, new livestock markets and covered markets, schools, churches, football grounds, hospitals and asylums, water pumping stations and sewerage plants totally altered the urban scene, and the country's population tripled with more than seven out of ten people being born in or moving to the towns. The century that followed, leading up to the Millennium's end in 2000, was to be a period of even greater change.

When Queen Victoria died in 1901, she was measured for her coffin by her grandson Kaiser Wilhelm, the London prostitutes put on black mourning and the blinds came down in the villas and terraces spreading out from the old town centres. These centres were reachable by train and tram, by the new bicycles and still newer motor cars, were connected by the new telephone, and lit by gas or even electricity. The shops may have been full of British-made cotton and woollen clothing but the grocers and butchers were selling cheap Danish bacon, Argentinian beef, Australasian mutton and tinned or dried fish and fruit from Canada, California and South Africa. Most of these goods were carried in British-built-and-crewed ships burning Welsh steam coal.

As the first decade moved on, the Open Spaces Act meant more parks, bowling greens and cricket pitches. The First World War transformed the place of women, as they took over many men's jobs. Its other legacies were the war memorials which joined the statues of Victorian worthies in main squares round the land. After 1918 death duties and higher taxation bit hard, and a quarter of England changed hands in the space of only a few years.

The multiple shop – the chain store – appeared in the high street: Sainsburys, Maypole, Lipton's, Home & Colonial, the Fifty Shilling Tailor, Burton, Boots, W.H. Smith. The shopper was spoilt for choice, attracted by the brash fascias and advertising hoardings for national brands like Bovril, Pears Soap, and Ovaltine. Many new buildings began to be seen, such as garages, motor showrooms, picture palaces (cinemas), 'palais de dance', and ribbons of 'semis' stretched along the roads and new bypasses and onto the new estates nudging the green belts.

During the 1920s cars became more reliable and sophisticated as well as commonplace, with developments like the electric self-starter making them easier for women to drive. Who wanted to turn a crank handle in the new short skirt? This was, indeed, the electric age as much as the motor era. Trolley buses, electric trams and trains extended mass transport and electric light replaced gas in the street and the home, which itself was groomed by the vacuum cleaner.

A major jolt to the march onward and upward was administered by the Great Depression of the early 1930s. The older British industries

– textiles, shipbuilding, iron, steel, coal – were already under pressure from foreign competition when this worldwide slump arrived. Luckily there were new diversions to alleviate the misery. The 'talkies' arrived in the cinemas; more and more radios and gramophones were to be found in people's homes; there were new women's magazines, with fashion, cookery tips and problem pages; football pools; the flying feats of women pilots like Amy Johnson; the Loch Ness Monster; cheap chocolate and the drama of Edward VIII's abdication.

Things were looking up again by 1936 and new light industry was booming in the Home Counties as factories struggled to keep up with the demand for radios, radiograms, cars and electronic goods, including the first television sets. The threat from Hitler's Germany meant rearmament, particularly of the airforce, which stimulated aircraft and aero engine firms. If you were lucky and lived in the south, there was good money to be earned. A semi-detached house cost £450, a Morris Cowley £150. People may have smoked like chimneys but life expectancy, since 1918, was up by 15 years while the birth rate had almost halved.

In some ways it is the little memories that seem to linger longest from the Second World War: the kerbs painted white to show up in the blackout, the rattle of ack-ack shrapnel on roof tiles, sparrows killed by bomb blast. The biggest damage, apart from London, was in the south-west (Plymouth, Bristol) and the Midlands (Coventry, Birmingham).

A W.H.Smith shop front in Beaconsfield, 1922.

A CENTURY of CARLISLE

Postwar reconstruction was rooted in the Beveridge Report which set out the expectations for the Welfare State. This, together with the nationalisation of the Bank of England, coal, gas, electricity and the railways, formed the programme of the Labour government in 1945.

Times were hard in the late 1940s, with rationing even more stringent than during the war. Yet this was, as has been said, 'an innocent and well-behaved era'. The first let-up came in 1951 with the Festival of Britain and there was another fillip in 1953 from the Coronation, which incidentally gave a huge boost to the spread of TV. By 1954 leisure motoring had been resumed but the Comet – Britain's best hope for taking on the American aviation industry – suffered a series of mysterious crashes. The Suez debacle of 1956 was followed by an acceleration in the withdrawal from Empire, which had begun in 1947 with the Independence of India. Consumerism was truly born with the advent of commercial TV and most homes soon boasted washing machines, fridges, electric irons and fires.

The *Lady Chatterley* obscenity trial in 1960 was something of a straw in the wind for what was to follow in that decade. A collective loss of inhibition seemed to sweep the land, as the Beatles and the Rolling Stones transformed popular music, and retailing, cinema and the theatre were revolutionised. Designers, hairdressers, photographers and models moved into places vacated by an Establishment put to flight by the new breed of satirists spawned by *Beyond the Fringe* and *Private Eye*.

In the 1970s Britain seems to have suffered a prolonged hangover after the excesses of the previous decade. Ulster, inflation and union troubles were not made up for by entry into the EEC, North Sea Oil, Women's Lib or, indeed, Punk Rock. Mrs Thatcher applied the corrective in the 1980s, as the country moved more and more from its old manufacturing base over to providing services, consulting, advertising, and expertise in the 'invisible' market of high finance or in IT.

The post-1945 townscape has seen changes to match those in the worlds of

Children collecting aluminium to help the war effort, London, 1940s. (*IWM*)

A street party to celebrate the Queen's Coronation, June 1953. (*Hulton Getty Picture Collection*)

BRITAIN: A CENTURY OF CHANGE

work, entertainment and politics. In 1952 the Clean Air Act served notice on smogs and pea-souper fogs, smuts and blackened buildings, forcing people to stop burning coal and go over to smokeless sources of heat and energy. In the same decade some of the best urban building took place in the 'new towns' like Basildon, Crawley, Stevenage and Harlow. Elsewhere open warfare was declared on slums and what was labelled inadequate, cramped, back-to-back, two-up, two-down, housing. The new 'machine for living in' was a flat in a high-rise block. The architects and planners who promoted these were in league with the traffic engineers, determined to keep the motor car moving whatever the price in multi-storey car parks, meters, traffic wardens and ring roads. The old pollutant, coal smoke, was replaced by petrol and diesel exhaust, and traffic noise.

Fast food was no longer only a pork pie in a pub or fish-and-chips. There were Indian curry houses, Chinese take-aways and American-style hamburgers, while the drinker could get away from beer in a wine bar. Under the impact of television the big Gaumonts and Odeons closed or were rebuilt as multi-screen cinemas, while the palais de dance gave way to discos and clubs.

Punk rockers demonstrate their anarchic style during the 1970s. (*Barnaby's Picture Library*)

From the late 1960s the introduction of listed buildings and conservation areas, together with the growth of preservation societies, put a brake on 'comprehensive redevelopment'. The end of the century and the start of the Third Millennium see new challenges to the health of towns and the wellbeing of the nine out of ten people who now live urban lives. The fight is on to prevent town centres from dying, as patterns of housing and shopping change, and edge-of-town supermarkets exercise the attractions of one-stop shopping. But as banks and department stores close, following the haberdashers, greengrocers, butchers and ironmongers, there are signs of new growth such as farmers' markets, and corner stores acting as pick-up points where customers collect shopping ordered on-line from web sites.

Futurologists tell us that we are in stage two of the consumer revolution: a shift from mass consumption to mass customisation driven by a desire to have things that fit us and our particular lifestyle exactly, and for better service. This must offer hope for small city-centre shop premises, as must the continued attraction of physical shopping, browsing and being part of a crowd: in a word, 'shoppertainment'.

A CENTURY of CARLISLE

Millennium celebrations over the Thames at Westminster, New Year's Eve, 1999. (*Barnaby's Picture Library*)

Another hopeful trend for towns is the growth in the number of young people postponing marriage and looking to live independently, alone, where there is a buzz, in 'swinging single cities'. Theirs is a 'flats-and-cafés' lifestyle, in contrast to the 'family suburbs', and certainly fits in with government's aim of building 60 per cent of the huge amount of new housing needed on 'brown' sites, recycled urban land. There looks to be plenty of life in the British town yet.

Carlisle: An Introduction

In AD 78–80 the Romans under Agricola established a base near the Solway Firth and called it Luguvalium. From that distant beginning Carlisle grew to become England's largest city covering 398 square miles (1,035 sq kms). Its borders stretch to Scotland in the north, the Solway Firth in the west, the North Pennines to the east and southwards almost to the Lake District. It has the highest point of any English city, Cold Fell at 2,041 ft (622 m) above sea level and the lowest, the sea level itself on the Solway Firth shore. It is the only English city not included in Domesday Book because in 1086 it was still part of Scotland. For more than 1,800 years, many of them turbulent, Carlisle played a prominent part in English history, being at the centre of the border troubles, and it was the last place in England to know peace. So when this fine historic city entered the twentieth century it was already well steeped in the rich fabric of history.

Carlisle made an innovative entry into the twentieth century. In January 1900, horse-drawn buses ceased running, superseded on 30 June of that year by electric tramcars operating from their London Road depot. They remained in business until 21 November 1931 and, when they ceased operating, Carlisle Corporation attempted to take over the undertaking. They were hoping to establish a municipal transport service, but were refused permission to do so by the Northern Traffic Commissioner. Ribble Motor Services of Preston became the principal operators and remain so to this day.

Children catching minnows near Eden Bridge, Carlisle, 1906.

Other horse-drawn vehicles continued to be used in Carlisle during the early years of the twentieth century. In 1904 a horse-drawn fire engine was purchased and, in 1909, a horse-drawn ambulance which also served as a black maria. However the development of the petrol engine meant the beginning of the end for most horse-drawn vehicles.

One of the areas in which the horse has remained king is the sport of kings. Carlisle's original racecourse was on the Swifts but when, in 1904, the lease expired the owners refused to renew it. So a farm was purchased at Blackwell, two miles south of the city centre and Carlisle's present racecourse was built there. It was on this racecourse that, in July 1929, the tote was used in England for the first time. The week following the last Saturday in June is annually when the main races are held and this has long been a public holiday.

Shaddongate United does not slip easily off the tongue. At a meeting on 1 May 1904, the shareholders of the football team bearing this name changed it to Carlisle United. The first FA Cup-tie the newly named team played was against Workington on 4 October 1904, on the Millholme Bank ground. In 1905 the team then moved to Devonshire Park and in 1909 it played its first game at Brunton Park, which it purchased in 1922. In 1928 Carlisle United was elected to the Football League and in 1965 it was promoted to the Second Division. It is now in the Third Division.

Another notable change occurred at Carlisle in 1904. Carlisle Education Committee, which had taken over from the old School Board, opened the Robert Ferguson School which was Carlisle's first council school. This marked the beginning of local authority responsibility for elementary education. In 1914 this was extended to include higher education. In 1970 the Robert Ferguson School closed as a secondary school. From then on Carlisle's education became completely comprehensive.

Before the century was a year old, Carlisle City Council had ventured into housing – a momentous move destined to improve the living standards of thousands of Carlisle folk. In 1900 the city council built thirty one-bedroom and ten two-bedroom flats to re-house working-class people as part of a Bridge Street slum clearance programme. But it was not until 1919, when the housing subsidy was introduced, that the building of council houses really took off. Between then and 1938 more

Once a familiar sight in Carlisle, the wood wagon coming along cobbled Charlotte Street is *en route* to the Nelson Bridge timber yard. The driver is giving the horses a breather before they tackle the slope ahead.

AN INTRODUCTION

than 5,000 new council houses were built in several parts of the city. More than half the population of Carlisle now lives in council property, the highest proportion in relation to population of any town in the country.

Prior to 1756, when Carlisle's first brewery was set up on the River Caldew, a tributary of the River Eden, the locals brewed their own beer. At the beginning of the First World War there were four breweries serving the city, all near the Caldew, collectively brewing 18,500 barrels annually. There were 119 licensed houses within the city alone. Brewing was big business.

In 1915 the Ministry of Munitions built a munitions factory near Gretna. Many navvies were employed during its construction and then many munitions workers were lodged in Carlisle. Highly paid and away from home, they sought solace in drink. The Central Control Board (Liquor Traffic), seeing that prohibition was not the answer opted for the state purchase of all but two of Carlisle's licensed premises. The Crown and Mitre Hotel and the County and Station Hotel. The Board closed fifty-eight of the pubs and, in 1916, took over the four breweries and closed two of them.

The Central Control Board became the Carlisle and District Management Scheme and was known as such until 31 March 1973, when it was sold off. Some of it went to various independent breweries as job lots, good and bad pubs being lumped together, some to private individuals. There are now sixty-six licensed premises in the city, so there is still ample choice.

Today Carlisle is a proud manufacturing city, home to several nationally and internationally known firms like the biscuit people, Carrs of Carlisle; the Metal Box Co. Ltd, who make containers; Cowans, Sheldon and Co. Ltd, who specialise in harbour, dockyard and railway installations; the Penguin Confectionery Co. Ltd, who make medicated lozenges and 'Nip its' and that world renowned civil engineering giant, Laings.

Carlisle's first newspaper, the *Carlisle Patriot*, dates from 1815. The Carlisle Conservative Newspaper Co. took it over in 1865 and, in 1910, the name was changed to *The Cumberland News*, which took over the *Carlisle Journal*. Today it is published weekly. Its sister paper, the *Evening News and Star* is published every evening.

Today the BBC takes good care of the spoken word while BBC North West is its TV outlet. Well-established Border TV provides an exciting, highly professional channel.

Carlisle's cathedral is smaller than many of its southern counterparts but more beautiful than most. During its history it was rebuilt several times but, by the grace of God, escaped being spoiled by the Victorians' passion for 'improving'. Despite being close to the busy Town Hall Square, it retains an air of solitude.

Carlisle's castle encapsulates all the turbulence of the Border Wars. The original building was a palisaded wooden structure built on a mound overlooking the Eden by William Rufus as a defence against the Scots. A Norman motte and bailey castle superseded it. King David I of Scotland captured the castle, enlarged and extended it and, in 1153, died there peacefully. It was the English King Henry II (1155–89) who built the stone keep, the castle's oldest remaining part, and its curtain wall. The most capable of medieval kings, the first Edward, nicknamed Longshanks and 'the hammer of the Scots', held the first Parliament in England in the Great Hall of Carlisle Castle in 1307. On 7 July of that same year he died of dysentery near Burghbysands on the Solway marshes and a monument marks the spot. This dour building has been besieged nine times by the Scots and re-captured four times. In 1745 Bonnie Prince Charlie captured it, briefly, before the English re-took it, since when it has remained in English hands.

The most attractive part of Carlisle is in the vicinity of the cathedral – where the Deanery with its sixteenth-century pele tower, the almost unspoiled Georgian Abbey Street and Tullie House built in 1689 and described by Pevsner as 'the most ambitious house in Carlisle' – make an exquisite assemblage.

A short walk along Castle Street from the cathedral will bring you to the traffic-free centre with its market cross, erected in 1682. Here the pleasantly restored Guildhall, which in the middle ages was the headquarters of the eight crafts guilds which formed the city corporation, the town hall, built in 1669 and extended in 1717, along with other splendid eighteenth- and nineteenth-century buildings, bring a touch of gentility to this lovely city.

Carlisle is proud of its past but does not live in it. This thriving picturesque city has become an important communication centre, being superbly served by road, rail and air. Moreover, its private industry has been matched by the public sector to such an extent that it has become a worthy capital of England's most beautiful region, Cumbria.

In 1985 its prestigious Lanes shopping centre was voted the best in Great Britain and its excellent Sands Centre Sport and Arts complex, on the bank of the beautiful river, attracts many business people because of its first rate facilities for conferences and exhibitions. The Sands Centre also promotes a variety of professional entertainment, catering for all tastes.

Carlisle had an uneasy birth and a rough upbringing. Yet it has defied the odds by developing into a capital city. It is an ugly duckling that has become a swan.

The Decade of Privilege

The twentieth century dawned on a society based on privilege and obsequiousness. People were expected to touch their caps to show their respect for their superiors – the squire, the vicar and the doctor. Not everyone was able to vote; it was a privilege reserved for men over a certain age and with some wealth. Elaborate social codes determined relations between people of different sex and rank. It was a world built on Victorian values of hard work and thrift; and it looked like it would last for ever. Britain was the greatest democracy in the world and, for the most part, its people were proud of their Empire. For this little Carlisle girl, having her morning wash in 1900 the future was an, as yet, unopened Pandora's box. Her smile was still of innocence.

A CENTURY of CARLISLE

Big wheel at Carlisle's annual fair, 1900. Show people, like the local Taylor family, became well-known in the city and their roundabouts pumped hurdy-gurdy music into the night, attracting huge crowds. 'Roll up, roll up', was the cry. 'They call us Taylor, not nailer'. Usually the centre piece was the merry-go-round with its prancing horses moving rhythmically up and down, their gleaming brass poles powered by magnificent traction engines, a harmony of hissing steam and polished brass. People sauntered around this surreal environment, moving from roll-a-penny to coconut shy and from shooting gallery to visiting side shows as fancy took them.

In this picture, also taken in 1900, a flamboyant barker exhorts a large crowd to 'come inside and be entertained as you have never been entertained before by these lovely lady wrestlers. See the strong woman lift a horse – this fine animal here, ladies and gentlemen, and all for the give-away price of two pence. Come along, folks it is a gift, "a doog hgual".' The words 'a doog hgual' are pure William Mounsey, the 'Jew of Carlisle', who frequently inscribed his name in the red sandstone of the Eden Valley backwards and Latinised. These words, read the right way round, become 'A good laugh'.

20

THE DECADE OF PRIVILEGE

In 1871, Phineas Taylor Barnum (1810–91) started a vast travelling circus which became known as Barnum and Bailey's. It came to Carlisle fair in 1900 and some of the animal's cages, pictured here, are parked near the Turf Hotel.

Charlie Chaplin visited Carlisle for the first time in 1904, the same year that the famous Indian scout, Buffalo Bill, was a main attraction on Carlisle's fairground. Here he is pictured, thin as a beanpole, taking part in a farce. In this production, one of his curvaceous assistants is wearing a patriotic Stars and Stripes skirt. That August the Lowther Arcade was opened and the following month, on 15 September, HM Theatre suffered a very serious fire. The theatre was not re-opened until 14 September 1905.

A CENTURY of CARLISLE

Around 1900, Carlisle was an important market for Irish geese. Those pictured here against a background of Eden Terrace and Eden Bridge, Carlisle, were brought by ship from Ireland to Silloth from where they were walked to various districts. They arrived in Silloth in groups of between 6,000 and 8,000 birds. Those destined for Carlisle were sold on in lots of between a dozen and thirty, the farmers who had purchased them walking them to their own farms for Christmas.

Carlisle's market in 1900 was sited in front of the Town Hall. The fine clothes worn by the elegant ladies and the gentleman in the top hat put them firmly among the upper echelons of Carlisle society. A fine Victorian pillar box is sited to the rear of the stalls, the first pillar box to be erected in England.

THE DECADE OF PRIVILEGE

Carlisle's new covered market was opened in 1901 and became an immediate success with local shoppers as this picture shows.

The Scotch Street entrance to the covered market, *c.* 1901, and the sun is shining brightly. Yet the lady in black crossing the cobbled street thinks it might rain and is taking no chances. The gas lamps were said to be the finest in England.

A CENTURY of CARLISLE

A view across Carlisle market place and along Scotch Street taken in 1909. The town hall is clearly seen in the background where originally a moot hall stood. This was replaced in 1669 by the first town hall, which was subsequently rebuilt in 1717 as the present one. The nearby Guildhall was built by Richard de Redness and was originally known as Redness Hall. The pillory was sited in front of the town hall and the stocks were last used in 1827. They are now housed in Tullie House, one of Cumbria's finest museums. The Victorian pillar box, the 33 ft (10 m) tall Carel or market cross and Steel's monument are all clearly seen. Obertelli's ice cream barrow – it can be licked but not beaten – is to the right of the Newtown tram.

Carlisle's duck and poultry market, pictured here in 1904, was in Lowther Street.

24

THE DECADE OF PRIVILEGE

'Yan, tyan, tethera, methera, pimp'. There are slight variations from dale to dale, but the ancient dialect way of counting sheep remains the same today as it did when Cumbria was part of the Kingdom of Strathclyde in the 'dark ages'. The shepherd in this photograph, taken in 1904, is driving Herdwick ewes over Eden Bridge and would have used this method of counting his flock. Some of the sheep will end up as an important part of a 'merry neet', the main ingredient of a tatie pot supper – the most tasty ones are always made with Herdwick mutton. Note the tramlines on the bridge.

A father and daughter discussing plants in Carlisle market in 1908. Perhaps they are thinking, 'shall we call the ornament holding the flowers a vase or a varse?' It all depends on how haughty their culture is.

25

A CENTURY *of* CARLISLE

The message boy, as he was called at the beginning of the twentieth century, is window gazing in St Alban's Row. The oyster shop sold fresh oysters every morning. The Old King's Head is just beyond the oyster shop and the town hall clock is prominent.

As a good means of advertising their wares, Robinson Bros, cash drapers, used the horse-bus. Here it is, *c.* 1900, outside Coledale Hall Farm, Newtown, Carlisle, its driver resplendent in top hat, whip at the ready. The fare was 2*d* inside and 1*d* on top.

THE DECADE OF PRIVILEGE

Queen Victoria died in January 1901. She was Empress of India and ruled over a quarter of the world, half a billion people. Her reign had been long and glorious and had lasted sixty-four years. At her funeral two emperors, two kings, twenty-four princes and thirteen dukes followed the gun carriage carrying her coffin while thousands of mourners stood in silence. In Carlisle on 26 January 1901, crowds gathered in the market place, braving the rain, to witness the proclamation of Queen Victoria's successor, Edward VII. Within twenty years most of those who had ridden behind her coffin had lost their crowns.

In July 1902, thousands of people gathered to watch the unveiling of a memorial to Queen Victoria. The day was fine and the crowd was well behaved and appreciative, as this picture shows.

A CENTURY *of* CARLISLE

Carr's Biscuit Works, Caldewgate, a major employer of local labour, is famed for its quality products, biscuits, confectionery and mill flour. In this picture, taken in the early 1900s, horse-drawn wagons of mill flour are leaving the premises. Carr's are a hygiene-conscious firm and always have been. Even their wagon drivers were issued with white jackets at the turn of the century. It fairly takes the biscuit!

Carr's employees spilling out of the works at knocking off time. All except one young lady, who is late for work.

THE DECADE OF PRIVILEGE

Cumberland and Westmorland hiring fairs were held twice-yearly at Whitsun-tide and Martinmass, the most important of them being at Carlisle, Cockermouth, Kendal, Keswick and Ulverston. At these most anxiously awaited fairs, those farm hands and servants not 'stopping on' for a further six months offered themselves for hire in the open market place. A straw stuck in a labourer's hat indicated that he was for hire and, once negotiations between a master and man were completed, hands were slapped and the man received a shilling as a token of a binding agreement. This shilling was called 'arles' or 'earnest money'. From the labourer's point of view, a 'good grub shop' was an important factor, while the master was seeking a hard working, dependable man of sober disposition. Women were hired in the same way. This emotional picture shows two girls being hired in Carlisle city centre in 1904. The farmer's wife is handing over the binding 'arles'.

Sometimes life can be just too much. Even the steps of the market cross can be as alluring as an eider-down pillow when you are worn out and need an afternoon rest period. This picture dates from about 1906.

29

A CENTURY of CARLISLE

In 1901 the Cumberland and Westmorland Yeomanry returned home to Carlisle from South Africa. Lord Lonsdale, 5th 'yellow' earl, pictured here in the dark coat, left of centre, leads the welcome. Born Hugh Cecil Lowther, Lord Lonsdale of Lowther Castle owned coal mines in West Cumberland. He was a well known horseman, boxer and yachtsman. As president of the National Sporting Club he laid down rules of boxing and presented the Lonsdale belts which have been awarded to British professional champions since 1909.

Carlisle Voluntary Fire Brigade, c. 1900, and its new steam engine. The last fire it attended was at Morton's Carpet Factory in December 1914. The man standing second from the right on the photograph is Captain James Little, the fire brigade's chief.

The Decade of Patriotic Fervour

The century is ten years old and the River Eden flows serenely under Eden Bridge, passing whitewashed cottages and Eden Terrace. It is Cumbria's longest river and to William Henry Mounsey, the 'Jew' of Carlisle it was Ituna, the fairest of all rivers, a view shared by the authors. Even in urban Carlisle *c.* 1910, there are foraging geese on it, bringing a touch of pastoral peace to a river that has grown old gracefully on its journey to the Solway Firth.

A CENTURY of CARLISLE

In 1910 people would saunter down Scotch Street to Rickergate Brow, perhaps to make a purchase from Jardine Carruthers & Sons, ironmongers, or to slake a thirst. On the right side of Rickergate Row there were thirty pubs from top to bottom. Now they have all gone and not one building seen in this photograph, taken c. 1910, remains.

St Cuthbert's Church, Blackfriar's Street, is built on the site of a building erected in AD 870 to house the body of St Cuthbert, a purpose for which it was never used. The site was chosen because it was there that St Cuthbert, who did so much to promote the spread of Christianity to pagan England, and St Herbert, who lived a hermit's life on an island on Derwentwater, first met. Throughout their lives they remained close friends. Both holy men died on the same day in AD 687 in fulfilment of a prayer by St Herbert. The Normans replaced the original building with a sturdier one which, in turn, was replaced by the current church in 1779. The railings surrounding the church, pictured here c. 1911, were erected to deter body snatchers.

THE DECADE OF PATRIOTIC FERVOUR

High Moor House, c. 1911. In 1745, the Young Pretender, Charles Edward Stuart, entered Carlisle and proclaimed his father King James VIII of Scotland and King James III of England from the market cross. By the end of December the city had surrendered to his purser, the Duke of Cumberland. While in Carlisle, the Duke stayed at High Moor House where Charles had stayed the previous month and slept in the same bed the Prince had used. To the left of the picture is John Strong's Ceylon Tea Warehouse.

Carlisle's county jail began as a dungeon in Carlisle castle and when the outer gateway of the castle was built in 1378, it incorporated the city's first built-in prison. Public hangings were a popular form of entertainment during the early part of the nineteenth century with thousands of people packing English Street to watch. Some of the prisoners were hanged in the street, others being executed on the prison wall. In this picture taken c. 1911, Carlisle jail is on the left and a delivery of beer is being unloaded outside the Jail Top public house.

33

A CENTURY of CARLISLE

It is c. 1910 and the Court Houses make an impressive backcloth to Carlisle's horse-drawn taxi cab ranks, conveniently situated close to Citadel railway station. The fares vary between 3d and 6d.

The same Court Houses some three years later, c. 1913, seen from a different angle, looking along English Street towards the Jail Top. Where once there were only horses, now petrol driven vehicles can be seen. A model-T Ford dominates the picture.

THE DECADE OF PATRIOTIC FERVOUR

Horse racing took place on the Swifts from the time of Elizabeth I until 1904 when the lease expired and the owners refused to renew it. Seen here is one of the last horse races ever run on that course. Imagine the excitement and the commentator's words: 'In the lead is Connie Lad by Yellow Earl out of Carlisle Lady and, trailing is the trainer by the railings out of breath.' Carlisle's present racecourse is at Blackwell, south of the city centre.

Seven years later, Carlisle's old racecourse became involved in a different kind of sport: the Daily Mail Air Race of 1911, when it became one of the stops, Carlisle Control. Here one of the contestants, a Mr Valentine, is shown on his aircraft at Carlisle Control on 26 July of that year.

A CENTURY of CARLISLE

Technology, a great new force, was beginning to change people's lives and the flight around Great Britain in 1911, sponsored by the Daily Mail, was one aspect of this trend. Here, Colonel Cody's aeroplane is shown on the Old Racecourse near the Turf Hotel, Carlisle, on 26 July 1911.

A fine example of those magnificent men in their flying machines, Colonel Cody, pilot of the above aeroplane, is pictured here signing autographs near the Turf Hotel on 26 July 1911.

THE DECADE OF PATRIOTIC FERVOUR

For a lot of us kids, 1911 was a happy year. Times without number we played in the River Eden near Eden Bridge, just off Victoria Park, where the water was shallow and the riverbed was sandy. It was safe there, and the sand found its way between our toes while we paddled. We would kick the current, scattering shoals of pin heads and minnows and slap the surface making splashes. We got our clothes wet and the grown-ups looking after us told us to stop it or else; but, oh, what fun we had! What glorious, innocent fun, with these simple pleasures! We wanted it to last forever.

In 1911 Great Britain was enjoying a period of peace and the future looked rosy. Here, on 24 June 1911, Carlisle sweethearts Mary Frances Parker and Dan Templeton are seen with relatives on their wedding day.

37

A CENTURY of CARLISLE

Ring a ring of roses,
A pocket full of posies,
Asha. Asha, all fall down.

A simple game that has delighted children since medieval times. Yet behind the seemingly innocent words lies a warning that the Black Death, a form of bubonic plague, could make them all fall down and die. These young Carlisle girls, playing the game in Victoria Park, *c.* 1913, are blissfully unaware that another killer, perhaps more potent than the black death, is imminent – the first war that was to suck civilians into it.

A troop of Westmorland and Cumberland Yeomanry is seen here, *c.* 1913, crossing the River Eden on Eden Bridge. Within a year some will have crossed the River Styx.

THE DECADE OF PATRIOTIC FERVOUR

All the seeds of the twentieth century, including democracy, equal rights and peaceful prosperity had been sown before the First World War, which swept away empires, crippled both the victorious and the defeated and left a legacy of hate. In 1914, going to war was seen as an adventure. 'Come into the ranks and fight for your King and Country – don't stay in the crowd and stare. You are wanted at the front. Enlist today.' urged the enlistment posters and many thousands did, not realising how warfare had been transformed in recent years. Early on the morning of 1 July 1916, the first day of the Somme offensive, the first waves of British soldiers climbed out of their trenches and advanced towards the German lines. The Germans climbed from their deep bunkers and opened fire. The well-disciplined British troops moved steadily across no-man's land to almost certain death. A German gunner recalled 'you didn't have to aim, you just fired into them'. The battle lasted four months and more than a million soldiers were killed or wounded. The soldiers pictured here at Murrell Hall, Carlisle, in July 1916, escaped that slaughter. They had been wounded earlier, were now hospitalized and, for the time being, out of the war.

By the summer of 1918 the German general staff realised that the war was virtually over and that they had lost it. By October they had marched their armies, in good order, back into Germany. On the eleventh hour of the eleventh day of the eleventh month in 1918, the fighting ended. When the ceasefire was declared in Britain the church bells of London rang out. In Carlisle, rejoicing people packed the streets. In this picture the people are in Bank Street. The London, Liverpool and Midland Bank is on the left.

39

A CENTURY *of* CARLISLE

It was as if nature was weeping for the war dead. The big flood of 1918 followed incessant heavy rain that caused the River Eden and its tributaries to burst their banks. This was the scene at the Water Works, Pettoril Bridge showing both the River Eden and River Pettoril unable to contain the tremendous force of the flood water.

The war which many in 1914 had thought of as an adventure had become a nightmare. It had lasted for four years during which time 65 million men, many little more than boys, had been subjected to discomfort, misery and terror. Almost nine million of them had died and each death represented a bitter tragedy for a family deprived, a wife widowed, a child without a father. Those who came back brought with them their injuries, their rage, their contempt for a once revered authority. They were determined that this should not be allowed to happen again. In every city, town and village in the country Peace Parties were held. Almost every street in Carlisle held one. Shown here is one held in William Street, off Butchergate, in 1919.

The Bitter-Sweet '20s

Among English cathedrals only Oxford is smaller than Carlisle, which was once larger than it is today. In 1133 Henry I made Carlisle the seat of a bishop and the priory then became Carlisle Cathedral. The south transept and the nave, now the Border Regiment Chapel, are about all that remains of the original building. During the Civil War, Carlisle was the chief Royalist stronghold in the north. Parliamentarians laid siege to it for eight months, the longest siege in the city's history. As the siege developed, Parliamentarian troops demolished six of the cathedral's bays and used the stone to repair the city walls and the castle. The truncated nave was later walled off and was still in poor repair in 1797 when Sir Walter Scott was married there. Much of the restoration work carried out by the Victorians was done with great sensitivity. The stars on the cathedral's blue ceiling are the work of Owen Jones who also replaced many of the coats of arms of local families that were originally on the medieval roof.

A CENTURY of CARLISLE

As the new decade, called by some the Roaring Twenties, by others the Jazz Age or the Treacherous Twenties, developed, people wanted to rebuild their lives, put the pain of war behind them and make the most of the peace. Among the well-to-do, the new thing was to be modern, to challenge everything. Jazz became the rage and lively dances accompanied it. Independent, hard working women abandoned layers of long, smothering garments in favour of simple clothes. Councils were democratically elected. This picture shows members of Carlisle Council leaving the old town hall following a council meeting, c. 1922.

During the immediate postwar years, war memorials were erected in cities, towns and villages throughout the land in honour of those who had made the supreme sacrifice during the First World War. One was unveiled at Carlisle, on 25 May 1922, by Lord Lonsdale in Rickerby Park. It commemorated all the fallen from Cumberland and Westmorland and the solemn occasion was well attended as this picture shows. Archie Creighton was the then Mayor of Carlisle.

42

THE BITTER-SWEET '20s

Come war or peace, certain members of our society need constant support and, thankfully, some dedicated people are there to provide it. Shown here, in 1922, staff of the workshops for the blind at Carlisle pose for a photograph.

'White flowers, white flowers, will you buy one of my white flowers? It's a good cause if ever there was one. Help us now and we'll help you when you're poorly.' These Queen Alexandra's Imperial Nursing Service (QAINS) nurses are busy fundraising in Carlisle, c. 1922.

A CENTURY of CARLISLE

Lifeboat Saturday in the 1920s. The lifeboat was sailed from Silloth to Sandsfield, from where it was hauled the four miles to Carlisle by a team of horses. At the end of the day it was returned to Silloth the same way.

A man with his travelling bear used to entertain the people of Carlisle and the surrounding villages in the 1920s.

THE BITTER-SWEET '20s

A tram coming up London Road on Carlisle's south-east side, towards the tram depot. The year is 1924, a very special one for Carlisle City Council. In September of that year the Council was able to use an official coat of arms for the first time ever. The previous year, 1923, the College of Arms informed them that the city arms they were using had never been registered. New arms were quickly drawn up, registered and recorded by Letters Patent. These arms are the ones in use today.

Carlisle's earliest arms date from 1462. On them were depicted a red cross on a golden field with four red roses and a fifth central rose in gold. The red roses were probably adopted in honour of the Virgin Mary, whose emblem they are and to whom Carlisle cathedral is dedicated. These arms were used from 1462 until 1835 when the reformed corporation adopted a new shield. This showed a 'lion couchant', which represented the lion of England. Below it was a castle which is a heraldic device indicating a city, and below that wavy lines represented a river. The whole shield signified 'an English city standing on the banks of the river'. These arms were used until 1924 when Carlisle City Council was informed that the city arms had never been registered. The arms used from 1924 onwards are shown here and comprise the original shield (centre), topped with a castle below which are two red wyverns with roses on their wings and the motto, 'Be just and fear not', which is taken from Cardinal Wolsey's speech to Cromwell from Shakespeare's *Henry VIII*, Act 3, Scene 2.

> 'Be just and fear not:
> Let all the ends thou aim'st at be thy country's,
> Thy God's and truth's.'

The arms stand on a green field.

45

A CENTURY of CARLISLE

The tram lines along Newtown Road near Coledale Hall in 1925 indicate a lessening of the dependency on horses. The Green Dragon pub is just along the road.

By 1924, traffic crossing Eden Bridge had increased more than somewhat. Now, as well as sheep and trams, there is an ever increasing volume of new-fangled motor cars.

THE BITTER-SWEET '20s

In 1925 the fitting shop of Hudson Scott and Sons had a day out to Ullswater and their vehicle, pictured here, was guaranteed not to have a puncture en route: it had solid tyres. In the twenties the hemlines of dresses rose and fell and rose and fell again. Breasts came and went and waists crept up and down the torso and sometimes vanished altogether. The man in the street was more interested in the shape of a lady's legs, be they in silk, artificial silk or even cotton lisle. In 1922 Carlisle's jail closed forever and F.W. Woolworth & Co. Ltd bought the site. In 1923 the first husband and wife team to be city councillors were Mr and Mrs Sewell. They became Mayor and Mayoress in November of that year making Mrs Sewell the first Mayoress who was also a serving councillor.

The Hudson Scott trip to the lakes was a success. Others decided that they would go there, too, only in more comfort. Their vehicles have pneumatic tyres.

A CENTURY of CARLISLE

Carlisle City police being inspected in the covered market, c. 1928. Batons at the ready, this formidable force is quite capable of administering the law of the land. Gathering crowds will be watched most carefully for signs of trouble.

Methodists moving from Caldewgate Methodist Church to their new church on Wigton Road, c. 1927–8. Any sign of trouble and the police may have to use their batons.

48

The Necessitous '30s

In the glorious years from 1933 until 1943, Revd George Bramwell Evans, *Romany* of the BBC, became the most popular of all children's broadcasters. He was born in Hull in 1884, son of a 'gorgio' (non-gypsy), and a 'romanichais' (gypsy woman). He entered the Methodist ministry and moved to Carlisle as minister of a small Methodist Chapel in September 1914. One day, while in Manchester, someone recognised him and the consequences of this meeting were to have a profound effect on the whole nation. Under the pseudonym *Romany*, with *Lullaby of the Leaves* as his theme tune he brought the countryside into the homes of city children who had never seen a blade of grass, and in so doing became an institution. He bought a *vardo*, a gypsy caravan, for £75 at Brough Hill Fair, which was pulled by a horse called Comma (because it seldom came to a full stop) and all his dogs were cocker spaniels and were called Raq. The first of his *Romany* books was published in 1937 and was an immediate success. A stone monument at Old Parks Farm in Glassonby, fashioned as a bird table, marks where his ashes are scattered. 'He loved the birds and trees and flowers and the wind on the heath.'

A CENTURY of CARLISLE

While *Romany* was roaming the Eden Valley lanes and back roads in his vardo gathering background material for his magical *Out with Romany* programmes (see page 49), many Carlisle people were being carried around that fair city in tram cars like the one shown here at the corner of Warwick Road and Lowther Street, *c.* 1930.

Not all the Carlisle trams were double deckers. This Denton Holme tramcar, pictured in 1931, was a single decker because its route took it under Denton Holme railway bridge, which was a low one.

THE NECESSITOUS '30s

For more than 200 years itinerant 'Scotchmen' had regularly visited the suburban areas of Carlisle, and the surrounding isolated farmsteads and remote dales, selling calicoes, printed cotton cloths, pins, buttons, braids and tapes. No matter what their nationality, they were always called 'Scotchmen'. During the twentieth century they switched from carrying bales of cloth to carrying pattern books and they always found a warm welcome as did the knife sharpeners, one of whom is pictured here in 1930. As well as sharpening knives he sharpened scissors and saws.

In 1930 milk was delivered by milk float like this Eskdale Creamery horse-drawn one. The milk was carried in churns and ladled into any suitable container the customer had to hand, pint and half pint ladles being used to measure it out. Here Willie Mallinson of Beaver Farm, Carlisle, and milk lad James Templeton are on the float while James's mother has her basin at the ready. The cost of a basin full of milk varied from 2d to 3d depending on the size of the basin.

51

A CENTURY *of* CARLISLE

Milkman Willie Mallinson and his brother, family butcher Jack Mallinson, were typical of Carlisle's small-business people during the 1920s and 1930s. They had regular customers who remained loyal year in, year out. Business relationships invariably developed into long lasting friendships. It was common practice, certainly until the Second World War, for people of a certain religious faith to purchase their provisions from someone of the same faith, usually from the same church or chapel. In the days before refrigeration, many customers would refrain from buying their weekend joint until late on the Saturday evening when the butcher would reduce what meat he still had rather than risk the likelihood of it 'going off'. It was not uncommon for butchers to remain open until midnight on a Saturday during the 1920s and 1930s. Most butchers had their own slaughterhouses and either did their own killing or hired a slaughterman.

Many people liked to vary their meals with a pheasant or two and some River Eden salmon or trout. This is where businesses like Robert Strong came into their own. He had a gun and fishing tackle shop in Castle Street, pictured here, *c.* 1930. He was skilled at making fishing nets and artificial flies and would advise on the type of artificial fly to use given the condition of the water at that time. The Rivers Petterill and Caldew flow into the River Eden in Carlisle and he was conversant with all three. An unusual feature about Robert Strong's shop is that half of it is used by an American dentist!

THE NECESSITOUS '30s

Mrs Hanah Parker, grocer, is pictured at the entrance to her shop in 1932. As well as the usual, ubiquitous groceries she sold products peculiar to the locality like Whillimoor Wang, a blue or skim-milk cheese. It was called a wang because it was possible to make wangs or leather-like shoelaces from it. A sign in Carlisle market described the cheese as 'lank and lean but cheap and clean'.

Coal from Lord Lonsdale's West Cumbrian coalfields warmed Carlisle in the 1930s. Here, in 1935, coalman Dan Snowdon is pictured with a wagon load of it, already bagged, but this is not a normal delivery. This is something special, perhaps a competition. In the shafts of the wagon a shire, resplendent in spit-and-polished equipment and adorned with ribbons, stands proudly while admiring householders look on.

53

A CENTURY of CARLISLE

John Menzies & Co. Ltd is not sharing any old railway station with Oxo, Bovril and Nestlé advertisements. This is Carlisle Citadel station, c. 1935, and it once had seven different railway companies operating from it. Sir William Tite built it in 1847 and its approach looks rather like a Tudor Manor house.

English Street with shoppers, c. 1930. With reference to the lady with the bicycle in the centre foreground, people walk tall in Carlisle.

THE NECESSITOUS '30s

On the world scene the financial collapse, that began with the Wall Street crash, triggered the economic depression of the 1930s, which threw millions of people out of work. In 1932 the League of Nations, in an effort to reduce the threat of war, belatedly organised the first disarmament conference in Geneva because the rise of extremism in Germany and of militarism in Japan were threatening peace. The League formally criticised Japan for invading Manchuria in 1931; and it left the organisation. Hitler came into power in 1933 and took Germany out of the League. In Carlisle, children cocooned by their innocence from world affairs continued to enjoy events such as this delightful May Day procession to St James's church, c. 1934.

In 1935 Italy invaded Ethiopia. The League of Nations failed to deal with dictators in Africa and, in 1936, Germany began to rearm. While this was going on, Carlisle was much involved with a big housing programme. Old Belle View village was built during the 1930s and some of the new dwellings are shown on the left.

A CENTURY of CARLISLE

The first time HRH Princess Louise visited Carlisle was in 1877 when she opened the viaduct. On 24 September 1908, she made a return visit, this time to open new wards in the Cumberland Infirmary. This picture shows her passing along Castle Street in procession returning from the opening of Lowther Castle, near Penrith. Her escort in the open carriage is flamboyant Lord Lonsdale, the 'Yellow Earl'. In those days, political parties in different constituencies had identifying colours of their choosing. The Westmorland Conservative Party's colour was yellow, Lord Lonsdale's favourite colour.

The Cumberland Infirmary was further improved by the opening of a new children's ward, c. 1936.

THE NECESSITOUS '30s

A fine Saturday afternoon at Carlisle's riverside cricket field in the thirties. The River Eden flows past one side of the fenced field and from the other side a grassy bank rises to make a natural grandstand. It is one of the most beautifully sited cricket fields in the country.

Cumberland and Westmorland wrestling, Bitts Park, *c.* 1927. The traditional dress of the contestants is a sleeveless vest, 'long johns' and velvet trunks, often elaborately embroidered. The skill of the event has more to do with balance and agility than brute strength. They 'tek hod', then sway drunkenly as they size each other up. Then, suddenly, the tempo increases as, in a flurry of flying feet, one will try to catch the other off guard and throw him so that a part of his body other than his feet touches the ground. Norsemen are thought to have brought the sport to Cumbria and it is on record that, in 1256, William of Gospatric had his shin broken in a wrestling bout.

A CENTURY of CARLISLE

This picture, taken in 1938, shows members of Fusehill Bowling Club, Carlisle, displaying the prizes they have won. Bowls is a very competitive sport, and today as many ladies as men play it, many buying their own sets of woods. The game starts with a small bowl, a jack, being pitched from a mark and two opponents, or opposing teams, take turns to roll wooden bowls towards it, the object being to finish as near the jack as possible.

Whatever the sport – be it cricket, Cumberland and Westmorland wrestling, bowls or any other – some of its most ardent fans re-live every detail of every contest over a jar or two in the 'public'. It is a ritual in many Carlisle pubs. Here, pictured in the 1930s, are the staff of Carlisle Brewery at the Old Brewery, Caldewgate, Carlisle, where the beer that stimulates the vocal cords is produced.

THE NECESSITOUS '30s

With the increase in the volume of traffic during the 1920s and early 1930s Carlisle's road system became increasingly congested and Eden Bridge was particularly badly affected. One solution to the problem was to widen the bridge, and work commenced in 1932. Here, pictured that year, steel fixers are working on the arches.

This picture of the Eden Bridge clearly shows how the widening work is progressing.

59

A CENTURY *of* CARLISLE

This picture, taken in 1936, is of a teacher and her class of spick and span infants at Norman Street Junior and Infant school. Primary education went up to the age of eleven years and most pupils left school aged fourteen.

Pupils outside Lowther Street school during the 1930s. The building has since been demolished.

The Violent '40s

In Carlisle, 1940 saw the demise of the Carlisle Otter Hounds after seventy-seven years as the most effective otter hunters in England. During its long and active life, Carlisle Otter Hounds was led by some brilliant hunters, of whom Thomas Dickinson Parker, pictured here in 1880, was the best. He was a master stonemason by trade but became a full time huntsman later in his life. This verse from the poem *Tom Parker: Huntsman* (1889) puts him firmly in the same league as John Peel with his foxes.

> Have you seen the bold Tom Parker?
> Have you heard his bugle horn?
> Have you seen the bold Tom Parker?
> With his hounds at early morn.
> Yes I've seen the gallant huntsman
> And I've heard the cheery hounds
> Ay' out Kirkandrews church:
> He's with the Carlisle Otter Hounds.

A CENTURY of CARLISLE

Between them the Carlisle Otter Hounds and the Dumfrieshire Otter Hounds hunted the Rivers Eden and Esk. During the seven years from 1903 until 1910, both Otter Hounds would hold a joint meet at Wetheral, a few miles upstream of Carlisle, to hunt the Eden, and at Longtown, just over the Scottish border to hunt the Esk. Together Carlisle and Dumfrieshire Otter Hounds had the two best packs of otter hounds in the world. They also had two of the most experienced huntsmen, brothers John Parker of the Carlisle Otter Hounds and Joe Parker of the Dumfrieshire Otter Hounds. Both were sons of the legendary Tom Parker. Both packs with some of their followers are seen here at Wetheral in 1903. The viaduct in the background carries the Carlisle to Newcastle railway across the River Eden.

It is 6.30 a.m. on a fine summer day, c. 1903 at Wetheral and the Carlisle Otter Hounds are about to begin a hunt along the River Eden. The huntsman in the centre of the picture, wearing a white waistcoat, is John Parker, Master of the hounds. John W. Graham is seen in the right foreground between two hounds, Dandie Dinmont terriers. All the hounds in the Carlisle pack were purebred otter hounds.

THE VIOLENT '40s

Here the Carlisle Otter Hounds are hunting the River Eden at Wetheral. On Friday, 30 July 1886, *The Carlisle Patriot* published a poem *Tom Parker and Carlisle Otter Hounds*. It is anonymous, nineteen verses long and begins:

> From Stanwix Bank Tom Parker's horn
> Peels through the morning air.
> And every sportsman in Carlisle
> Arises from his lair

If the stones of Carlisle castle could talk, what tales they could tell! Like for example the one about Sir Andrew de Harda who, with his 'Kendal archers, all in green' defended the castle against the onslaught by Robert Bruce in the fourteenth century. Bruce then set siege to the city but was unable to conquer it. In this picture, c. 1943, the castle looks at peace yet the country is again at war.

A CENTURY of CARLISLE

This Armstrong Whitworth Whitley long range heavy bomber is making an emergency landing at Kingstown airfield during the Second World War. It just managed to clear the road and fences.

The old road to the canal, c. 1943. It also leads to the Bond Store, Creighton's Saw Mill, the dog kennels, where Carlisle Otter Hounds were housed and the back entrance to Carr's Biscuit Factory. Where have all the people gone? They've been called up. Didn't you know, there's a war on.

THE VIOLENT '40s

Carlisle Co-operative Flour Mill's depot during the early forties epitomises the cheerless austerity of a country at war. Times were grim. Food rationing was introduced in stages, beginning cautiously on 8 January 1940, with bacon and butter being rationed at 4 oz per person per week and sugar at 12 oz per person per week. All householders had to register with their local shops. In March 1940, meat rationing was introduced based on price rather than weight. The cheaper the cut, the more meat was available.

In March 1941, the call-up of British women to help in the war effort was announced. Registration, of twenty and twenty-one-year olds, began in April 1941. Exceptions were made for pregnant women and mothers with young children. This caused an immediate drop in girls seeking domestic service as many women opted for the auxiliary services: Women's Royal Navy Service (WRNS), Women's Auxiliary Air Force (WAAF), or the Auxiliary Territorial Service (ATS). Others joined the Women's Land Army, worked in munitions factories, tank or aircraft factories, civil defence, nursing, transport and other key occupations, releasing men for the armed forces. In Carlisle's Holme Head textile mill alongside the River Caldew women filled the jobs of those male employees who had got their call-up papers.

A CENTURY of CARLISLE

The uniforms of the members of the Border Regiment, pictured in front of the portcullis at the entrance to their headquarters at Carlisle Castle in 1904, may have changed but the pride of this celebrated regiment remains steadfast. At the outbreak of the Second World War, the 1st Battalion of the Border Regiment served with the BEF in France. It then trained as part of the first Air Landing Brigade of the 1st Airborne Division from October 1941 until October 1945. The battalion moved to North Africa in May 1943, and took part in the first major Allied glider operation of the Second World War, the landing in Sicily on 9–10 July when, tragically, many lives were lost as gliders crashed into the sea. The battalion served in Italy, then played a significant and distinguished role defending the western side of the Division's perimeter at Oosterbeck near Arnhem in September 1944. In May 1945, it was sent to Norway to supervise the surrender of German forces. Lt Col Tommy Haddon was Commanding Officer, 1st Battalion, The Border Regiment, from July 1943 until September 1944. Under his leadership the battalion was one of the best units in the army. He had a tremendous interest in his regiment and was appointed President of the Border Regiment Association in the new King's Own Royal Regimental Association in 1975. A greatly respected man, he died in 1993 at the age of eighty.

THE VIOLENT '40s

In the small hours of 7 May 1945, German General Alfred Jodl signed an unconditional surrender. Hitler had committed suicide in his Berlin bunker a week earlier. Prime Minister Winston Churchill and US President Harry S. Truman agreed that the following day, 8 May, should be celebrated as Victory in Europe (VE) Day. That night the street lights of Carlisle, as elsewhere throughout Britain, were switched on and for the children who had grown up in the blackout it was like fairyland. Street parties were held, people rejoiced and in Carlisle services of thanksgiving were held in churches and in the cathedral. Two and a half months later the Japanese surrendered and Victory over Japan (VJ) Day was celebrated on 14 August. Britain had won the war: now it had to win the peace.

But what is peace? To many a Carlisle fisherman peace is trying his luck, like the fisherman pictured here, for brown trout in the River Caldew amid glorious scenery.

67

A CENTURY of CARLISLE

During the war everyone carried an identity card at all times, to be produced on demand. Civilians were issued with a ration book by the Ministry of Food, to be handed to the shopkeeper – who removed the coupons needed for the restricted foods – together with the appropriate sum of money. Rationing did not end with the war. Food remained scarce for several years after peace was declared and butchers in particular found themselves never short of friends. Pictured here, Mr Middleham, butcher, his son and daughter-in-law, Molly, are in their Newtown Road shop surrounded by a mouth-watering display of meat.

In this picture of English Street, c. 1948, all looks serene but most of the goods for sale in Binns and Marks & Spencer are still on ration and likely to be for some time.

THE VIOLENT '40s

The Crown & Mitre Hotel was built in the early 1900s. It replaced an earlier inn and coffee house of the same name which had stood on this site at one of Carlisle's two stagecoach stops. The handsome building was fortunate enough to survive the Second World War and is still operating as a hotel today.

A CENTURY of CARLISLE

Gardens at the Carlisle end of Rickerby Park, pictured here in the late 1940s, are a restful haven conducive to pleasant thoughts.

The view from the Italian gardens across manicured lawns to the River Eden, gliding between green meadows to its meeting with the Irish Sea on the Solway Firth, is ideally suited to romantics in love. This is a local monkey run (favourite haunt of lovers), one of many that abound in and around Carlisle; and Gretna, with its smithy where runaways in love tie the knot over its anvil, is just across the border.

The Teenage '50s

What a whopper! Over the years the River Eden has produced some big salmon. This fish was caught near Knockupworth Gill by James Templeton in 1954. It weighed an amazing 42½ lb. The same week a gentleman called Joe Taylor, a game keeper from near Armathwaite – a beautiful village upstream from Carlisle – also caught a large salmon. His weighed 43 lb.

A CENTURY of CARLISLE

The 1950s were called the teenage decade because it was then that the word 'teenager' was coined. There are some teenagers in this picture, taken in 1951, but don't strain your eyes looking for them. Use a magnifying glass. Port Road railway bridge is in the foreground, the building on the corner is the Jovial Sailor pub and Carr's biscuit factory is at the back. Most of the people are knocking off at the end of a shift.

HRH Princess Margaret paid a civic visit to Carlisle in 1951. Here she is seen accompanied by the Mayor of Carlisle, Councillor Routledge; the Chief Constable, William Lakeman; the Lord Lieutenant of the County and other dignitaries.

THE TEENAGE '50s

The deanery and part of the west wall. The building on the right is the Elim Church, now no longer there. This picture was taken in 1950.

This delightful young lady, pictured in 1958, is hoping to gain entry into Carlisle castle through the same postern gate featured in one of our best-known narrative poems. The poem in question brings out the flavour of this troubled 'Debatable Land' during the 170 years of Tudor sovereignty. It is the tale of William Armstrong of Kinmont, alias Kinmont Willie, one of the most notorious of the border 'Broken Men' or outlaws.

A CENTURY of CARLISLE

Teddy Roberts, seen here with his dog and his pram, was well known in the Newtown area of Carlisle during the 1950s. He collected rags.

Rationing of some foods continued until as late as 1954 but, by 1956 when this picture was taken, there were more provisions in the shops. Something in the Pioneer Stores' window has caught the eye of a couple of shoppers.

THE TEENAGE '50s

LONDON — CARLISLE SPECIAL. 29.9 MILES WITHOUT A STOP. JULY 19TH 1903 (L.&N.W. RAILWAY)

Speed was considered to be an essential part of the policy of competing railway companies until a series of nasty accidents occurred on curves at Grantham, Shrewsbury and Salisbury in 1905–6. These had the effect of hardening opinion, both within the railway system itself and with the general public, that acceleration in the 'race to the north' had gone far enough. This double-headed London to Carlisle special completed the 299 miles without a stop on 19 July 1903, thus creating an endurance record and paving the way for the much more powerful Coronation and Royal Scot locomotives half a century later.

Coronation Class No. 46239, 4–6–0, 'City of Chester' leaving Carlisle for London Euston, c. 1956.

75

A CENTURY of CARLISLE

Coronation Class No. 46252, 4–6–0, 'City of Leicester', coming towards Carlisle station, passing No. 3 signal box. Many, but not all, of this class of locomotive were streamlined. To accommodate the streamlining the original smoke box was sloped at the top. When the locomotives were re-built, the streamlining was removed and smoke deflectors added. The smoke boxes had to be rebuilt to their full height.

Coronation Class No. 46231, 4–6–0, 'Duchess of Atholl' is gathering speed as she pulls 'The Royal Scot' northwards out of Carlisle, driver Donald Sunderland at the controls. In 1949 the locomotive's livery was blue, then it was green and, in 1956, became red. The railside building is the old Carlisle slaughterhouse.

THE TEENAGE '50s

Coronation Class No. 46236, 4-6-0, 'City of Bradford', pulling the Royal Scot, is leaving Carlisle for Glasgow and has just passed under Caldew Bridge. The tall chimney in the background belongs to the brewery and Dixon's factory is seen far right. Coronation Class locomotives like this one were built from 1937 and not all were streamlined. Those that were had the streamlining removed from 1946.

The Britannia Class locomotive, No. 70053, 4-6-0, shown here standing in Carlisle station, is so new that it has not yet got a name. It was later named 'Moray Firth'. All these locomotives were taken out of service in 1964 and replaced by diesels.

A CENTURY of CARLISLE

'Roman' soldiers marching along Annetwell Street during the octo-centenary celebrations of the city in 1958. Some time between AD 78–80 Petillius Cerialis marched westwards over Stainmore to Carlisle. About the same time Agricola reached Carlisle en route to Scotland from Wales and it was he who established a base in Carlisle, which the Romans knew as Luguvalium. A garrison was based there while Agricola moved northwards, deeper into Scotland. The garrison lived in a turf and wooden fort which they built where the cathedral now stands.

This *tableau vivant*, part of the octo-centenary celebrations, depicts medieval Carlisle not as it was but as it should have been.

78

THE TEENAGE '50s

Gypsies taking part in the octo-centenary parade in July 1958, with their horse-drawn vardo (gypsy caravan) in Annetwell Street. You can tell that this bow-topped vardo was made in England because the chimney stack is always sited on the side of the vehicle away from the roadside, the better to avoid becoming caught in the overhanging branches of trees. Those built in Europe have their chimney stacks on the left.

This delightful picture of Mrs Templeton and her daughters, Frances and Elizabeth, was taken in 1959 on the West Wall at the deanery. It highlights the gentle face of this proud city. The Victorian gas lamps add charm.

A CENTURY of CARLISLE

A contrast in bridge styles. This is the North British Railway Bridge on the northern edge of Carlisle. It has electricity power towers for company and, when this photograph was taken during the 1950s, the old LNER coal loader shed, behind the bridge on the left, was still standing.

Closer to the centre of Carlisle, the Eden Bridge, wider now and without tram lines, is surrounded by trees and flower beds.

The Space Age '60s

On 23 May 1964, a beautiful clear day, James Templeton was on a quiet outing to the Solway Marshes when he took what he thought was a perfectly ordinary colour photograph of his younger daughter, Elizabeth, aged five. The film was handed to a local firm who sent it to the Kodak Colour Processing Laboratories for developing. When the film was returned, the assistant told James that one of the best pictures had been spoiled by the man in the background wearing a space suit. At first James thought she was joking but there it was – a spaceman, as this picture shows. James approached the Carlisle Constabulary about his amazing photograph and both film and print were forwarded to their forensic laboratories at Preston for examination by photographic experts. It was too good a photograph for the figure to have been caused by a blemish on the film and, anyway, James had been informed by Kodak that it was impossible for any exposure to be made on a new film before being sold. James was adamant that there were no trees or water reflections which could have interfered. The image of the man is definitely part of the negative. The nearest people to them when James took the photograph were an elderly couple, in a car reading a newspaper. A minute after he took that snap, James took another one of Elizabeth from almost the same spot and there was nothing unusual on it. The background was perfectly clear. This extraordinary story has been featured in UFO magazines and on national TV.

A CENTURY *of* CARLISLE

The spaceman picture was taken on Kodacolour X film at 100th of a second at F16. Here James and his wife, Anne, are inspecting the camera, a Pentacon Reflex with which the photograph was taken. Technical experts who examined the camera could find nothing unusual about it.

It is not unknown for salmon and trout to be poached from within the confines of the city of Carlisle from the Rivers Eden and Caldew. But as this picture, taken *c.* 1960, shows, poaching is not confined to fish. Here, the Guards are poaching – they call it recruiting – recruits from under the very noses of the Border Regiment. Damned cheek!

THE SPACE AGE '60s

Carlisle castle is home to the Border Regiment and has always been separate from the city of Carlisle. This view of the castle across Corporation Road, taken from high on a 100 ft turntable ladder in Carlisle's fire station yard, shows the great keep in prominent display.

The sally port steps and the west wall of the city looked better in 1965, when this picture was taken, than in 1522 when the Scots under the Duke of Albany were threatening to attack Carlisle. Lord Dacre, defending Carlisle, thought that the city walls were so ruinous that they would not be able to withstand a siege. He therefore arranged to meet Albany five miles north of Carlisle and bluffed him into retreating.

A CENTURY *of* CARLISLE

Today, and in 1960 when this picture was taken, Carlisle welcomes Scots – and any other nationality for that matter – and if the visitors have money to spend they will get value for it. There is a special reason for this. An article appeared in *The Citizen*, a monthly magazine, on 1 May 1830 which said that 'the natives of Carlisle are neither English, Irish or Scotch, but a mongrel breed between them'. It went on to call them 'incapable of friendship' and made other disparaging remarks, none of which held water. That is why the citizens of Carlisle are keen to welcome visitors like these back packers looking at the statue 'of William, Earl of Lonsdale. They want to put the record straight and show Carlisle as the beautiful, welcoming, capital city of the Lake District it is and themselves as the happy, warm-hearted, loveable people they are. Why, they even moved the statue of Lord Lonsdale from English Street, outside the jail, to its present site in front of the courts so that it could be better seen by visitors arriving by train. Then they pulled down the jail to show what a lovely lot they are. You can't get much more welcoming than that.

Much of Carlisle's humour transcends decades and is gentle and inoffensive. This humorous sketch of the drunk in English Street is likely to raise many a knowing smile.

84

THE SPACE AGE '60s

The sixties was a permissive decade with old and trusted standards being rejected by the advocates of the 'make love, not war' doctrine of groups like the flower people. How refreshing it is to find that postcards depicting happy innocence were still available in Carlisle during that period.

During the 1960s the wind of change was blowing around the world. Colonial territories were screaming for independence but, as freedom arrived, expertise left and civil wars and military takeovers followed in rapid succession. Carlisle's doves of peace, pictured here, were sadly missing in those emergent countries in the sixties and, in many cases, they still are.

A CENTURY *of* CARLISLE

This is Castle Street in the late 1930s, looking south, away from the castle. It looks so peaceful in the summer sunshine with not a cloud on the horizon. But storm clouds are gathering over Europe.

This is Castle Street in the 1960s, looking north towards the castle. It looks even better in the summer sunshine than it did in the late thirties and the storm clouds over Europe have dispersed.

THE SPACE AGE '60s

This brand new addition to Carlisle's police force arrived during the 1960s. Here police officers Dick Cowan and S. Millican inspect it for fingerprints.

PC Roger Milburn and Sgt R. Rutherford having a top secret talk at Abbey Street corner, c. 1960.

A CENTURY of CARLISLE

Here mother and daughter McBride put on an impressive show in Carlisle market where for a great many years they have sold flowers, fruit and vegetables. They are still in business now, with a travelling shop.

Cumberland Show, held annually in late July at Carlisle, is the largest agricultural show in Cumbria. It attracts thousands of people, many of whom are in some way involved with agrarian matters. Here young beasts, having been groomed for the occasion, are on parade.

THE SPACE AGE '60s

There was once a pond, Hammond's, in Carlisle's Upperby and, now cleaned and remodelled, it is a wildlife centre. Some of its inhabitants shown here in 1960 are seemingly living in harmony. The mute swans, which are not silent as their name suggests, are not hissing so they are not annoyed. The coot does not have its head lowered and its wings raised, so it is not being aggressive. One of the female mallards is happily feeding up-ended, and none of the drake mallards is showing any special interest in the opposite sex. It is an idyllic scene: too good to last.

West Tower Street looking towards East Tower Street and facing Lowther Street School. The school had its share of schoolroom howlers like the one by the pupil who was writing an essay on Carlisle. He wrote 'in the market there are several stalls where the butter women lay their eggs'. On another occasion, when a teacher asked 'why did the daughter of Herod ask for the head of John the Baptist?' a pupil replied, 'Please, sir, to mek broth on'. All these buildings have now gone; but the schoolroom humour remains in other schools.

A CENTURY of CARLISLE

This lovely scene of a railwayman cycling home was taken during the winter of 1969–70 and neatly joins the two decades. Shadows of trees in winter sunshine transform the walls of houses into works of art but a dusting of snow on the west walls of the city serve to remind that bleak winter still has an icy hold on Carlisle.

The Depressive '70s

Winter on Rickerby Park, Carlisle, 1969–70.

A CENTURY of CARLISLE

By the mid-seventies many people in the West had begun to assume that their new prosperity would last for ever. But the Middle East oil crisis shook Western confidence, precipitating recession and growing unemployment. This heralded the end of the boomtime age. In Carlisle, in 1975, the event that captured the imagination of the population was the Great Fair. Here, at 8 a.m. on 26 August 1975, the town clerk reads out the official Great Fair Proclamation from the carel cross in the market square.

Here are some of the people who crowded into Carlisle market square to hear the Town Clerk read the official Great Fair Proclamation, which was followed by a day crammed with a veritable abundance of fun and entertaining things to see and do. Many visited the Great Fair Open Market with its stalls, sideshows, flower girls and rudd women (selling the red stone used for polishing steps) re-creating Old Carlisle.

THE DEPRESSIVE '70s

Mr Scott, Parks Superintendent, accompanies the Mayor of Carlisle, Councillor T. Walley, resplendent in gorgeous Edwardian dress, between rows of dahlias and gladioli in Carlisle market during Fair Week.

There she is again, still in the covered market, now accompanied by other VIPs and the town crier.

A CENTURY of CARLISLE

Snakes alive! She probably also has a crocodile handbag! One of the ladies entertains the crowds during Carlisle's fabulous and highly successful Great Fair of 1975. She had to compete with free fall parachutists, the Red Arrows, the Royal Artillery Motor Cycle Team, continuity drill by the Queen's colour Squadron, RAF, a mock battle by Cumbria's Cavalry Regiment and so many more attractions. But was she daunted. Yes she was.

The year Carlisle's Great Fair was re-started was 1975 when Tom Bisland was Mayor. In 1982, during Donald Fell's term of office as Mayor, Anne Templeton, who looks absolutely delightful pictured here in the covered market, was Queen of the Great Fair. In 1983, much to the dismay of many Carlisle folk, and following what many thought was a daft move, Carlisle Council discontinued the role of Queen of the Great Fair. Such decisions can be revoked and it would be rather nice if this one was.

94

THE DEPRESSIVE '70s

The wonderful thing about Carlisle's Great Fair, as Mayor Councillor T. Walley and the exquisitely adorned VIP ladies seated alongside her in 1975 would have told you, is that it is now an annual event. It was established in 1353 and used to be proclaimed from the carel cross at 8 o'clock every 26 August. The custom lapsed, but, thanks to the enthusiasm of some determined Carlisle people, it was revived and has become firmly re-established.

A CENTURY of CARLISLE

I am thinking of you at Carlisle.

The very feminine dresses worn by the VIP ladies at the 1975 Great Fair are reminiscent of a gentler age which this postcard portrays. This pensive young lady, reflecting on what she has been reading, leads people away from the bustle of the twenty-first century back into a slower world, more in keeping with the seasons, where sometimes there was time for quiet reflection.

As you will see they're after me at Carlisle

Not everything changes. Aggrieved wives have threatened miscreant husbands since time immemorial. Dress vogues alter but the humour of the situation remains constant.

96

THE DEPRESSIVE '70s

In 1745 the 34th (Cumberland) Regiment fought a gallant rearguard action at the Battle of Fontenoy, for which it was awarded a Wreath. The 55th (Westmorland) Regiment served in China from 1841 to 1842 and for this they were awarded a Dragon superscribed with CHINA. In 1881 these two Regiments were amalgamated and became respectively the 1st and 2nd Battalions of The Border Regiment. The two awards are incorporated in the Border Regiment cap badge. This proud Regiment is seen here beating the Last Retreat in front of their home, Carlisle Castle.

This was Carlisle City Coat of Arms between 1885 and 1924, when a new coat of arms was drawn up, registered and recorded by Letters Patent. This was because the previous coats of arms had never been officially registered. This design, pictured in the late 1970s, depicts Carlisle exactly, but, not being officially registered, the symbols meant nothing. The coat of arms introduced in 1924 remains Carlisle's coat of arms to this day.

Carlisle town centre, now pedestrianised, has not only retained its old world charm, it has regained a tranquillity it lost with the coming of the petrol engine. The Old Town Hall looks better now than it did when it was first built in 1669. The contrasting architecture in the heart of Carlisle is exciting and far superior to the architecture of many other cities.

THE DEPRESSIVE '70s

A glorious summer day in the late seventies. The deep blue waters of the River Eden are gently flowing under the splendid Eden Bridge. The river bank is awash with cow parsley and, overhead, cotton wool clouds drift languidly across a pale blue sky. It is a peaceful pastoral scene. Yet it is in the middle of the city. That is part of the magic that is Carlisle.

Carlisle cathedral has a most attractive site and from its tower the views are long and good. This picture, taken in the seventies, is northwards to Carlisle Castle and the lovely wooded countryside beyond. The tall building, front centre, is Tullie House, 'the most ambitious house in Carlisle'. It was built in 1689, is Carlisle's only Jacobean building and today houses Carlisle's museum.

A CENTURY of CARLISLE

William Henry Mounsey of Rockcliffe (1808–77), the 'Jew' of Carlisle, was a most remarkable man and the great love of his life was the River Eden, parts of which he adorned with rock carvings. Seen here flowing benignly through Carlisle in the late seventies, Ituna, as he called it, is following a course different from the one it used some 400 years ago. At the southern end of Eden Bridge there are some stumps sticking out of the water among some large sandstone blocks. These are the remains of a temporary bridge built after the Eden changed course in 1571. Before then it flowed in a wide sweep close to the castle. Then, in January 1571, flooding caused a break in the river bank, shortening this sweep and forming a stream, Priest Beck. Wooden bridges crossed both the Eden and Priest Beck but by 1601 they were in ruins. Two stone bridges replaced them, the cost being met by the county because at that time this spot was not part of the city. Gradually the channels changed in importance until by the beginning of the nineteenth century, the Priest Beck had become wider than the main channel, which was then filled in. The name Priest Beck was dropped. Today, although only one bridge crosses the Eden at this point, local people often refer to it as 'the Eden Bridges'.

The Proud '80s

It is not surprising that Carlisle, all 398 square miles of it, includes some good fox hunting country. At places like Cold Fell, 'dragging' the fells to locate the scent begins in the early morning before the hunt starts. Once the scent has been picked up the hounds will follow their quarry for many miles across rough country, scrub, bog, scree and the like. Here the Cumberland Farmers Fox Hounds, a pack that began in the eighteenth century, is leaving Caldbeck. Huntsman Ted Norton is on the leading horse.

A CENTURY of CARLISLE

Towards the end of 1907 General Robert Baden-Powell visited Carlisle to inform people there about a new movement he was hoping to establish, the Boy Scouts. The next year the Boy Scout movement came into being. Two years later, 1910, he and his sister founded the Girl Guides for Girl Scouts and in the years that followed, both movements spread throughout the world. As a means of teaching fellowship and good citizenship, laced with adventure and founded on Christian principles, these two movements lead the way. With time, the uniforms have changed but not the ideals. Organisations like the Scouts and Guides produce those steadfast citizens that are the backbone of our society. Here the Wigton Road Methodist Scouts are taking a photo call, c. 1980.

Having allegiance to the Scouts and Guides and similar organisations is a matter of pride. Having allegiance to Carlisle's coat of arms, albeit an unofficial one in this case, by owning a splendid moustache cup like the one shown here, is also a matter of pride.

THE PROUD '80s

This winter landscape of Victoria Park would make anyone feel proud.
'I love snow and all the forms of radiant frost.'

Percy Bysshe Shelley, 1792–1822

A CENTURY of CARLISLE

Butchergate in the 1930s.

Now it has a more modern touch. Pride, you see! It is the talk of the town.

THE PROUD '80s

In 1983 HRH the Princess Royal opened Carlisle Leisure Centre, The Sand Centre, on 28 June. It is a sports and arts complex and attracts many business people because of its first rate facilities for conferences and exhibitions.

HRH the Duke of Gloucester opening the prestigious new Lanes Shopping Centre, 1987. That year it was voted the best shopping centre in Great Britain. A lot of the big chain stores have taken up residence there and won't budge. To the front from left to right, are Sir Charles Graham, Lord Lieutenant; Ron Wilson, Town Clerk; the Duke and Ian Stockdale, Carlisle's Mayor.

105

A CENTURY *of* CARLISLE

There is a pleasant ambience about the Lanes. It is almost a pleasure to overspend in a place like that.

Some people prefer the outside market and in such pleasant, floral surroundings who can blame them?

THE PROUD '80s

Carlisle Castle, pictured here in brilliant sunshine, is where Mary Queen of Scots was imprisoned in 1586. She used to walk, for exercise, on the area below the Castle's southern wall, which became known as Lady's Walk. She spent only two months there before being moved to Bolton Castle in Wensleydale which was considered to be a safer stronghold.

A CENTURY of CARLISLE

HRH The Prince of Wales receiving the Freedom of the City of Carlisle in the Council Chamber of Carlisle Civic Centre, 1986.

On the same visit HRH Princess Diana went on a walkabout and is shown here talking to members of the crowd.

108

THE PROUD '80s

In 1988, HRH Princess Alexandra (centre), as Colonel-in-Chief of the Kings Own Royal Border Regiment, visited them at Carlisle Castle. After lunch she visited the Regimental Chapel in the cathedral (above). The Queen's chaplain is to the left of HRH.

HRH Princess Alexandra in informal mood, chatting to James Templeton about photography and cameras.

A CENTURY of CARLISLE

It is a sunny day in 1988 and at the south end of Lowther Street, looking towards the Courts, the Town Crier, Billy Dixon, is looking anxious. Behind him the Scots pipers are at the ready. The crowds are gathering eager to raise a cheer or two for HRH Princess Alexandra. But where the devil is the Royal Lady? You've guessed it. She is still discussing photography and cameras with James Templeton.

Fin de Siècle

> Fair quiet, have I found here,
> And Innocence thy sister dear!
> Society is all but rude,
> To this delicious solitude.
>
> Andrew Marvell, 1621–78

The glory of Victoria Park, 1998.

A CENTURY of CARLISLE

The control tower of Carlisle airport in 1990.

Vulcan Bomber at Carlisle airport in 1990.

FIN DE SIÈCLE

Since it was built in 1847 by Sir William Tite, Carlisle railway station has been the scene of countless sad partings and joyous reunions. The great and the not so great, the high and the lowly have all passed through the impressive portal. In 1989, HRH, the Duchess of York, visited Carlisle and is seen here being met by the Lord Lieutenant, Sir Charles Graham. This was one of her first visits after becoming Duchess of York.

A CENTURY of CARLISLE

Fusehill hospital, Carlisle, c. 1976. In its early days this was regarded as the hospital for the poor; inside the design was unusual in that you could look down from one floor to another – as in a Victorian prison. Accommodation for tramps was provided in an outbuilding next to the hospital although they had to work in exchange for a night's keep.

Carlisle also has a city maternity hospital, pictured here. It is well run, well used and – well! – caters for tiny patients with a loud voice at one end and a complete lack of responsibility at the other. It shares the same building with Carlisle's two other hospitals, the complex being called 'The New Hospital'.

FIN DE SIÈCLE

Before 1904, when it became Carlisle United, the city's football club was called Shaddongate United. Millholme Bank was its home ground until 1905 when the team moved to Devonshire Park where this photograph was taken during the 1907/8 season. On 2 September, Carlisle United played its first match on Brunton Park, a ground it purchased in 1922.

Leading his team out of the tunnel on 20 August 1955 is Ivor Broadis, carrying the ball, followed by Vic Kenny, and for both of them this was their first season with Carlisle United. The third man is goalkeeper John Burn. The game is against Chesterfield, the first of the season, the result being a 1–1 draw.

115

A CENTURY of CARLISLE

Bill Green scores Carlisle United's very first goal in Division One. The match is against Chelsea at Stamford Bridge on 17 August 1974.

The Carlisle United team at the start of the 1995/6 season. Proudly displayed, front centre, is the 3rd Division Championship Cup for the 1994/5 season. Later in the 1995/6 season, Carlisle United played Birmingham at Wembley for the Autoglass Trophy and lost.

FIN DE SIÈCLE

It was Robert Nelson Burgess who brought the *East Cumberland News* into the modern age. In 1910 he amalgamated it with the *Carlisle Patriot*, bringing into being the *Cumberland News* as it is still known today. He also launched, in the early 1900s, the *Evening News*. Over the years, the company that owns *Cumberland News*, Cumbrian Newspapers, one of the very few independent family owned newspapers in the country, has created a loyal following from both readers and advertisers alike. This exclusive presentation of the Solway spaceman story of 23 May 1964, is a good example of the precise and lucid way the *Cumberland News* covers events. The heroine of the story is Elizabeth Templeton (see page 81).

Here Elizabeth Templeton, now Mrs Dobson, on the left, is shooting a feature about the spaceman for Border Television. Burgh Marsh is the site. Eric Wallace, Border TV presenter, is facing her. Director Bill Cartner is behind the camera and the lady with the hat is Thirly Grundy, production assistant.

117

A CENTURY of CARLISLE

At 5.45 p.m. precisely, on Friday 1 September 1961, Border Television was introduced to 400,000 viewers. It marked the culmination of a ten-year dream for Sir John Burgess, managing director of Cumbrian Newspapers. By 6 October of that year it was estimated that Border TV was being seen in 64,000 homes with the figure increasing daily. Its local programming is dominated by the very popular news magazine *Lookaround*, and one of the *Lookaround* team is Fiona Armstrong, pictured here, who joined Border TV in 1984.

FIN DE SIÈCLE

In 1968 the then head of Border TV gave the job of reporter/presenter to Eric Wallace, pictured here. He has been with Border TV for thirty-two years, latterly as a freelancer. He tells the story that, after thirty years on the box, he met an old school friend in a pub and rather grandly enquired, 'How are you, Bill?' Bill eyed him for a full minute before answering, 'Yer getting a queer gut on yer!' No matter! As good presenters, Eric and his colleagues have become synonymous with the high quality material Border Television presents.

Christmas is always a special time of year; and when it is the last one of the twentieth century, there is more than usual cause for reflection. Pictured here in the very heart of Carlisle, mid-December 1999, the figures in the Christmas tableau brighten a wet winter evening and cheer Christmas shoppers who are on the verge of a new century. An uncharted area for them, and others like them, to mould into what they would like it to be.

A CENTURY *of* CARLISLE

A new century is not always clearly defined. More often than not there is overlap, as this picture of Scotch Street taken from West Tower Street shows. It was taken in late December 1999, and shows cranes that were erected towards the end of the twentieth century ready for building work on Debenham's new store and multi-storey car park being built at the start of the twenty-first century.

The cathedral gives Carlisle its solid Christian foundation, the castle gives the city its roots, the River Eden its cohesion, Tullie House its history, the citizens its sense of humour and these cranes its sense of purpose.

The future of Carlisle can never be in any doubt. As Lakeland's greatest poet, William Wordsworth, put it, it is 'enough if something from our hands has power to live and act and serve the future hour'.

Acknowledgements and Picture Credits

The Templeton Collection houses probably the very best record in existence of yesteryear Carlisle and it is to Anne Templeton that we, the authors of this book, give our special thanks. Throughout its preparation, Anne, you have been unstinting in your devotion to fishing out pictures best suited to our needs – no easy task. So thank you, you are a real treasure. To the Worshipful the Mayor of Carlisle, Councillor Ray Knapton, our sincere thanks for your keen interest in this book which we hope does justice to your beautiful city. Dear Fiona Armstrong, many thanks for keeping us *au fait* with Border Television. Thank you, Elizabeth Templeton for your fascinating spaceman story and accompanying picture. We still think we earthlings are better looking than he is! David Steel, Carlisle United's historian, we salute you and wish the team you support every success. Thank you for your valued help. Thank you also *Eagle Graphics*, for the typing. To the brilliant editorial team at Sutton Publishing, Editor Simon Fletcher, Project Manager Fiona Eadie, Assistant Editors Michelle Tilling and Annabel Fearnley and PR specialist Joyce Percival our very special thanks. What a pleasure it is to be working with such lovely friends, happy in the knowledge that we all have the same end in view – a publication that maintains Sutton Publishing's very high standard. If anyone has been overlooked – hard luck! It is inadvertent and we apologise. Responsibility for any errors is shared between Charlie Emett and J.P. Templeton.

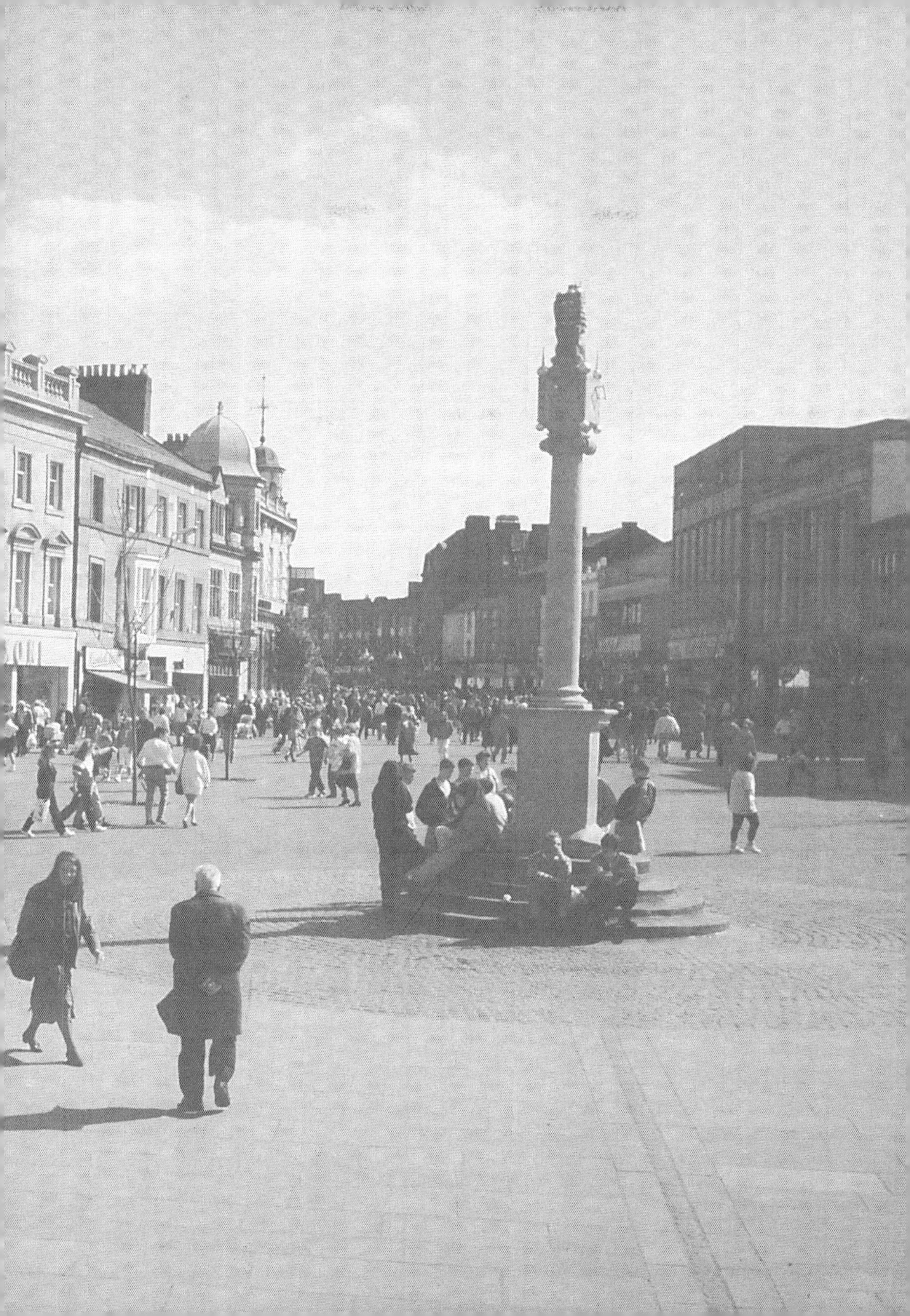